BIS

Please renew or return items by the date shown on your receipt

www.hertfordshire.gov.uk/libraries

Renewals and enquiries: 0300 123 4049

Textphone for hearing or 0300 123 4041
speech impaired users:

L32 11.16

Christmas
Festivals Around the World

Words in **bold** can be found in the glossary on page 24.

©2017
Book Life
King's Lynn
Norfolk PE30 4LS

ISBN: 978-1-78637-166-9

Written by:
Mike Clark

Edited by:
Charlie Ogden

Designed by:
Evie Wright

A catalogue record for this book
is available from the British Library.

Christmas

Festivals Around the World

When you see Sarah, she will tell you how to say a word.

What Is a Festival?

A festival takes place when people come together to celebrate a special event or time of the year. Some festivals last for only one day and others

Some people celebrate festivals by having a party with their family and friends. Others celebrate by holding special events, performing dances or playing music.

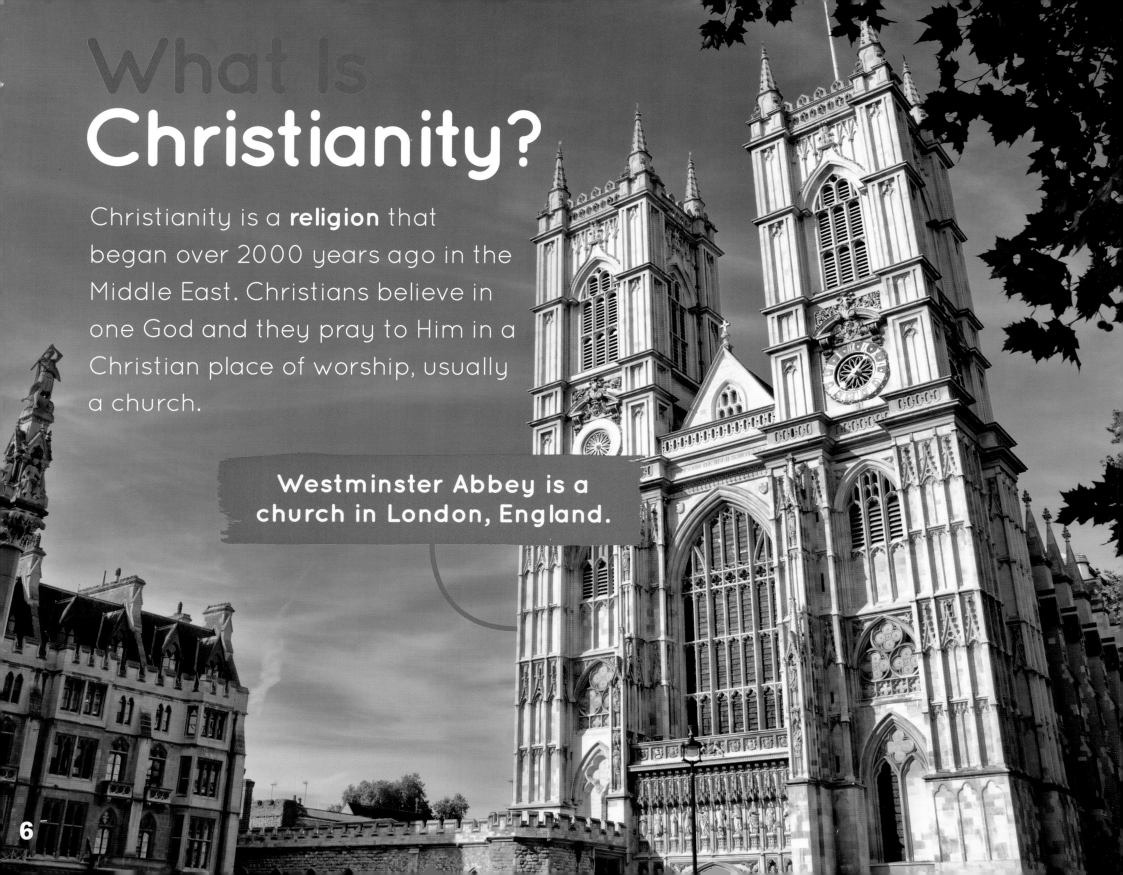

What Is
Christianity?

Christianity is a **religion** that began over 2000 years ago in the Middle East. Christians believe in one God and they pray to Him in a Christian place of worship, usually a church.

Westminster Abbey is a church in London, England.

Christians read from a holy book called the **Bible**. The Bible includes the word of God and it tells people how to lead good lives. Many people go to church to pray or to attend special **services**, which are usually lead by a priest or a vicar.

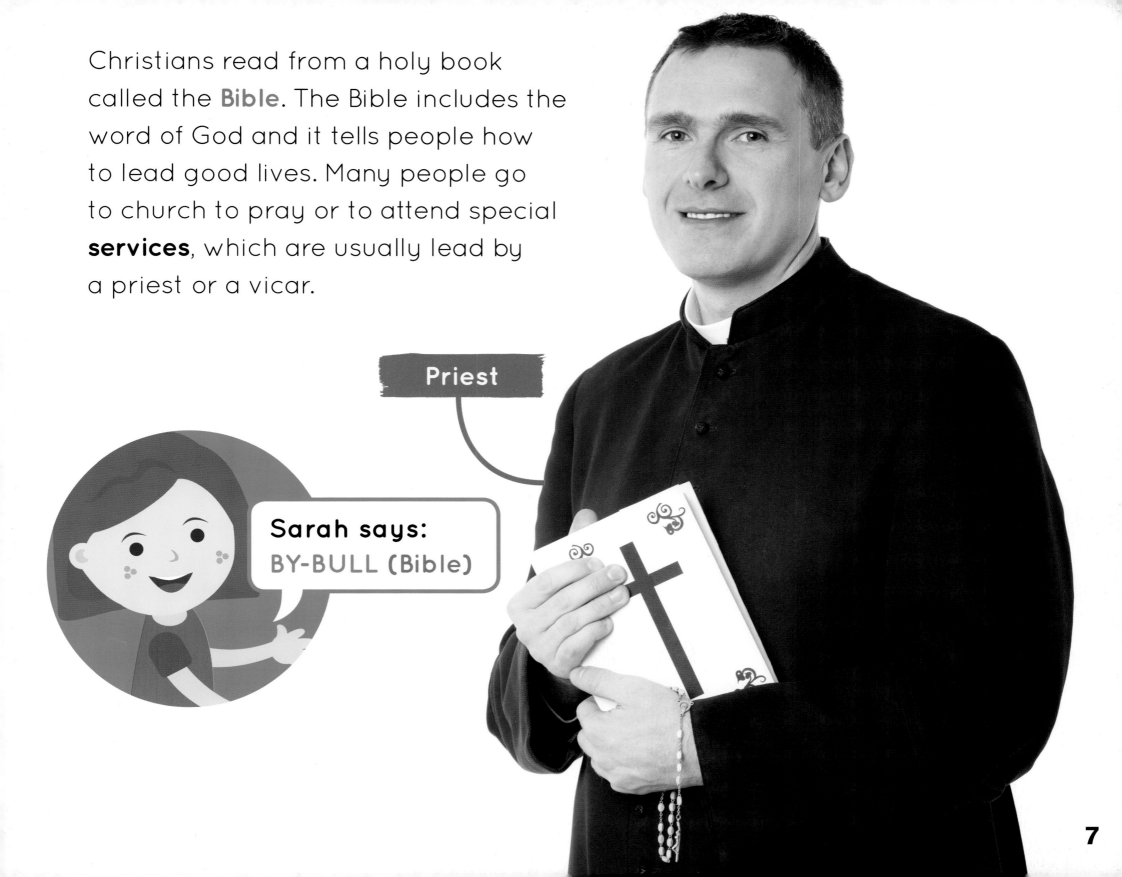

Priest

Sarah says:
BY-BULL (Bible)

What is Christmas?

Christmas is a Christian festival that is celebrated every year on the 25th of December. Christians believe that on this day, many years ago, Jesus Christ was born.

8

Jesus Christ is very important in Christianity. Christians believe that Jesus Christ was the son of God and that he helped to heal the sick and feed the poor.

Sarah says:
GEE-SUS CRY-ST
(Jesus Christ)

The Story of Christmas

The story of Christmas is about the birth of Jesus Christ. It is often called the **nativity** story. Over 2,000 years ago, God sent one of his angels to talk to a woman called Mary. The angel told Mary that she would give birth to Jesus Christ, the son of God.

Mary and her husband, Joseph, decided to go to a place called **Bethlehem**. On their trip, the tried to stay at an inn, but it was full. However, they were allowed to stay in the inn's stable. While they were in the stable, Mary gave birth to Jesus. The birth caused a new star to shine in the sky.

Sarah says:
BETH-LEE-HEM
(Bethlehem)
NA-TIV-EE-TEE
(Nativity)

Many children act out the nativity story in a school play just before Christmas.

Three wise men saw the new star and knew that it meant that a new king had been born. They followed the star and it led them to the stable where Jesus ha d just been born.

Later, an angel appeared to three **shepherds** and told them that a new king had been born nearby. The shepherds visited Mary and Joseph and told them that an angel had said that their baby, Jesus, was the **saviour** of the world.

Christians now celebrate Christmas every year because it is the day that Jesus Christ was born.

Prayer

Some Christians go to church. At church, a priest tells stories about the miracles that Jesus performed. Christians in church often worship Jesus by singing **hymns** and praying.

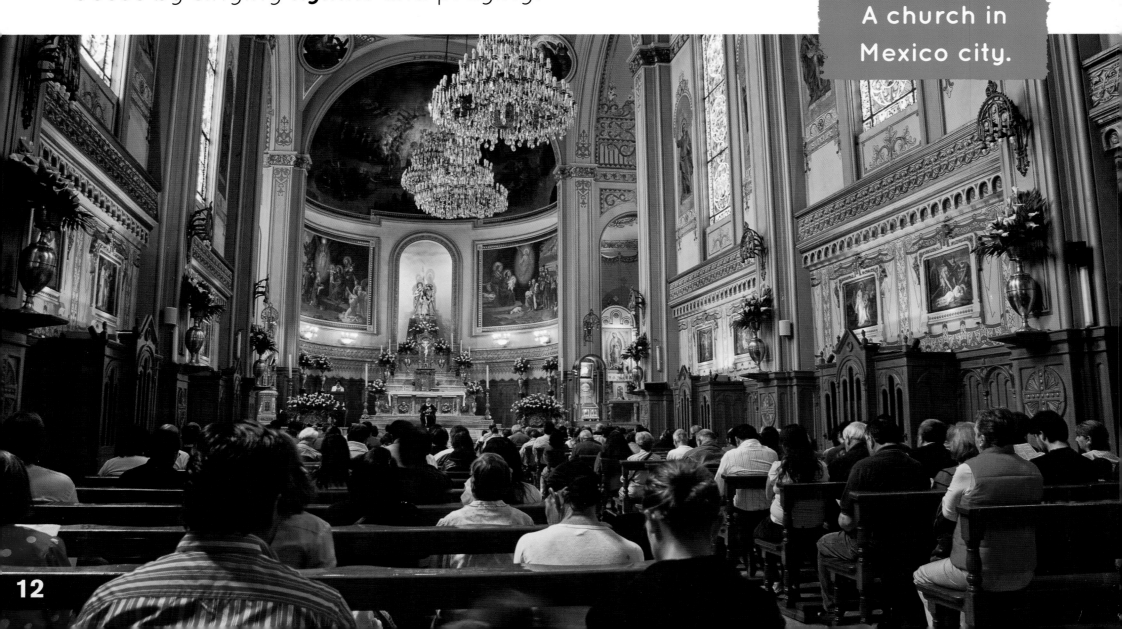

A church in Mexico city.

In the days before Christmas, many people like to sing **carols**. These people are called carollers and they often collect money to give to charity.

Santa Claus

Many children around the world believe in **Santa Claus**. Santa Claus is an old man who lives in the North Pole and loves Christmas.

Sarah says:
SAN-TA CLAWS
(Santa Claus)

On the night before Christmas, Santa Claus brings gifts to children who have been good. He rides a **sleigh** through the sky that is pulled by flying **reindeer**.

Decorations and Gifts

People who celebrate Christmas usually decorate a tree with **baubles** and **tinsel**. They also put bright lights around their house.

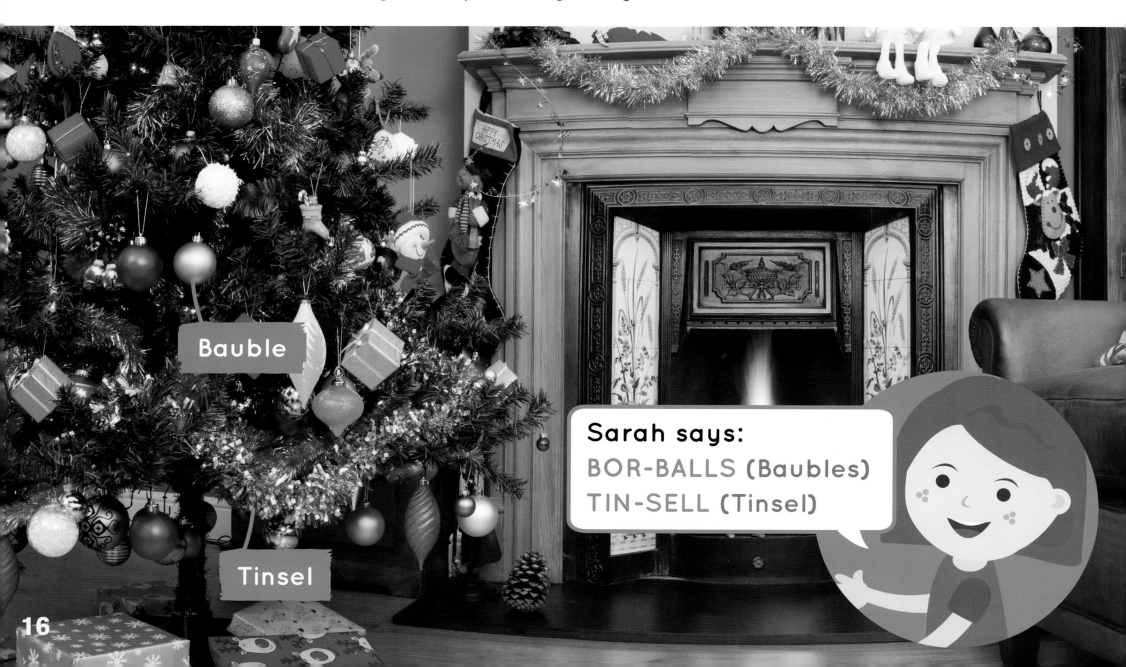

Bauble

Tinsel

Sarah says:
BOR-BALLS (Baubles)
TIN-SELL (Tinsel)

On Christmas day, Christians all around the world give each other gifts. Many also give away money to charity.

The gifts are also called presents.

Festive Food

Most families get together to eat a big meal on Christmas day. It is a Christmas tradition to eat turkey at this meal.

People also eat sweets and different types of cake. Many people also eat Christmas pudding, which is filled with fruit.

Charity

Christmas is a time for people to give to charity. Charities raise money so that they can help people.

At Christmas, many people give money to charities so that they can help people around the world. Some people also cook food and give away gifts.

Sarah Says ...

Bauble
"BOR-BALLS"
Round balls that are placed on Christmas trees as decoration.

Bethlehem
"BETH-LEE-HEM"
A very old city in the Middle East.

Bible
"BY-BULL"
The Christian holy book that contains the word of God.

Jesus Christ
"GEE-SUS CRY-ST"
The Son of God.

Nativity
"NA-TIV-EE-TEE"
The birth of Jesus Christ.

Reindeer
"RAIN-DEER"
A type of deer that usually lives in very
cold places.

Santa Claus
"SAN-TA CLAWS"
A man who loves Christmas and gives out
toys to children who have been good.

Sleigh
"SLAY"
A type of carriage that has blades
instead of wheels.

Tinsel
"TIN-SELL"
A long, shiny and fuzzy type
of decoration.

Glossary

carols Christmas songs

hymns religious songs or poems in praise of God

saviour a person who saves others

services times of prayer or worship at a church

shepherds people who look after sheep

Index

Credits

Photocredits: Abbreviations: l-left, r-right, b-bottom, t-top, c-centre, m-middle.
Front Cover: bg – mmkarabella, l – Gelpi, m – Veronica Louro r – Fotohunter, 2 – Aleksey Sagitov, 4 – Tom Wang,
5 – Monkey Business Images, 6 – r.nagy, 7 – Monika Wisniewska, 8 – Ugis Riba, 9 – Renata Sedmakova, 10 – Zvonimir Atletic,
11 – Zvonimir Atletic, 12 – M.V. Photography, 13 – 1000 Words, 14 – Milles Studio, 15 – Milles Vector Studio, 16 – Paul Maguire,
17 – Billion Photos, 18 – Subbotina Anna, 19 – Shebeko, 20 – Syda Productions, 21 – Wavebreakmedia, 23 – Iconic Bestiary
Images are courtesy of Shutterstock.com. With thanks to Getty Images, Thinkstock Photo and iStockphoto.